Endorsements

"We have read this wonderful book written by one of our dear Deacons at our parish. We are so blessed to have him. "Go in Peace" is a well-written, uplifting, easy-to-read book. It's thought-provoking and provides an insightful view into how he intertwines family and career to enrich his spiritual life, mixed with a nice touch of humor. It is definitely well worth the read!"

> **– Members of St. Pius X Rosary Group,**
> **South Yarmouth, Massachusetts**

"In writing *Go in Peace*, Deacon Tony shares a wonderful explanation of how prayer, Holy Mass and the Rosary guide you through your everyday life. With guidance from Deacon Tony's book my daily prayer life changed, and helped center me knowing God is by my side in everything I do."

> **– Kathleen J. Barrett, Administrative Assistant,**
> **Office of the Diaconate, Diocese of Worcester**

"A retired Firefighter/Fire Chaplin/Teacher Looks back on his years of service is a heartfelt journey through one's life that is well written and easy to read. Tony has elegantly

tied in how his faith in the lord has enriched his life experiences from childhood into adulthood…. Experiences
that range personally as a husband, father and friend to
many…professionally as a firefighter and a science
teacher, as well as spiritually as an ordained deacon in the
Catholic Church. The chapters flow beautifully. There is
great detail of his personal experiences that have deepened
his faith in the lord which has enriched his life as well as
the life of many others.   Brilliantly written, a must read."

**– Jim Clayton, Retired President/COO,
Target Securities, Member New York Stock**

"I've been around for a long time but have never met a
writer like Deacon Tony. I found this book to be extremely
interesting from a writer who talks from the heart and extremely cares about the good will of people. This story
tells about real love and feelings that Tony feels for others
and people he will never forget. God Bless you Tony and
please continue to write."

– Stephen Ring, former Professional Baseball Player

"GO IN PEACE"

May Our Lives Always Give Glory to God

A Retired Firefighter, Deacon, Fire Chaplain, Teacher, and Family Man Looks Back on His Years of Service

Dcn. Tony Surozenski

En Route Books and Media, LLC
Saint Louis, MO

⊕*ENROUTE*
Make the time

En Route Books and Media, LLC
5705 Rhodes Avenue
Saint Louis, MO 63109

Cover Design: Sebastian Mahfood
Copyright 2025 Tony Surozenski

ISBN: 979-8-88870-465-3
Library of Congress Control Number:
Available online at https://catalog.loc.gov

Phil. 4:13, "I can do all things in Him who strengthens me."

Table of Contents

Introduction

In his last two books, *Called to Serve: Life as a Firefighter-Deacon* and *The Roller Coaster Ride of Life: A Worthwhile Challenge*, the author of this book wrote about his experiences as a firefighter, a deacon, a chaplain, a teacher, and a family man. He had often asked himself if he was doing the firefighter thing for his own ego building or really for the greater glory of God. At times, did it also apply to the others? Maybe it was just part of normal life experiences in general? Time would tell.

In his early years, he thought that it was more about himself and what he could do that others couldn't. The reason is that not everyone was allowed to be a firefighter, and he could say to himself, in his mind anyway, "Look what I'm doing. Isn't it great? It's a respectable position, so don't ever look at me in a negative way." For the most part, people did look up to firefighters. They looked up to them for their bravery and for all that they would do to save lives and property. After all, as it has been pointed out by many, "These firefighters must be crazy because while everyone is running to get out of buildings, they are running in to them." So, in a way, it does build up one's ego. Being treated with dignity and respect is always a plus. However, as he grew in maturity, he realized that it wasn't just ego building; it truly was trying to do more for others who suffer from the tragedies of fires. As he looked back at those 24 years of service, he had also come to realize that all the people with whom he served were really about helping others. Okay, maybe some thought the way he did earlier on, but the privates, officers, and chiefs were genuine in their concern for the lives of people and property. Those were the underlying reasons why they all became firefighters.

The responsibilities of being a firefighter are great, and the training reflected that. From getting the turnout gear on quickly and safely, to donning an air pack properly, and handling the various size hoses, to setting up ladders properly and even positioning the apparatus along the streets, all had to be done in an expert manner. All was the result of initial training and months and years of continuous training.

Sure, the satisfaction of getting the fire out, saving property and people's lives is a real mind builder, but the relief of a job well done sets one's mind at ease and brings one down to realizing that we are all vulnerable and thanking God for a job well done.

Once in a great while, a fellow firefighter gets caught in a building and suffers from the effects of the fire. Thank God that injuries and deaths as a result of fires are not regular, every day occurrences. Those left behind suffer deeply from those situations. In the department that he served, there were some injuries and fortunately very few line of duty deaths. Loss of life is tragic no matter what the circumstances, but firefighters know what line of duty deaths entail, and that makes it worse to deal with mentally as the days go by. It's one thing to have sympathy for victims who die in a fire, and no words seem to bring comfort to the families and friends left behind, but it always is worse when your firefighter friend dies. Often, the "What ifs" pops into their minds. "Would things have been different if we only did this or that?" A blame game may also enter as well. Blaming oneself is the worst. It's after times like these that Critical Incident Stress Management teams are needed. They are held, hopefully, within 24 to 48 hours after the tragic incident.

The sessions really help, not only with line of duty deaths, but also when others succumb to death because of a fire or accident. The loss of adults is tragic, but it really bothers the first responders when a child is the victim. Often, tears flow profusely because of that tragedy, and it takes time to get back again to what some would call normal life.

This firefighter experienced the help of CISM teams over the years and noted such in previous books. It was because of those experiences that he became an instructor for some of the courses dealing with relieving stress and suicide prevention. He also thought that he grew deeper in his faith due to getting involved with those types of courses. He noted that because when he was ordained a Deacon in the Catholic Church, he felt that he would need to resign his position as Captain of Ladder 1 on the Webster Fire Department and focus more on Diaconate services in the parish that he would be assigned to. Fortunately, the Chief at the time said that he didn't want to lose him and had the Board of Fire Engineers appoint him as Fire Chaplain for the Department.

It was a few years later that he was introduced to the Massachusetts Corps of Fire Chaplains and from that point on he was able to serve and help others, which included their spiritual lives as well as their physical and psychological issues. Once again, it got him to thinking about how and why he was serving people. As he thought and prayed about it, he realized that he did move away from the ego aspect and more to the other aspect for the greater glory of God. As a Fire Chaplain, he was able to serve from 1990 to 2017 when he finally retired. Or so he thought. It turned out to be somewhat of a semiretirement because he would serve when local Chaplains for police and fire would be away on vacation or out of town for some reason. He thanks God for the rewarding service that still continues.

One may wonder what got him through the time of service as a firefighter and chaplain. At the end of his last book, *The Roller Coaster Ride of Life: A Worthwhile Challenge,* he listed several prayers and books that helped him along the way. The following sections will cover how some of those actually affected his service along with everyday interactions with his wife, family, friends, and people in general.

Helping Hands

As he looked back at his entire life and not just the years as a first responder, chaplain, and deacon, he noticed that he seemed to have been called to service of some kind at a very early age. He reflected on his childhood and how his parents brought him to church to be baptized, and, as he got older, on how they brought him to what is called Holy Mass. It is also known to many as Mass or a Eucharistic Celebration. He was always fascinated with the prayers, which were mostly in Latin, the songs, and with what some have called "the smells and bells."

When he expressed an interest in what the altar boys did, his parents let him go into a type of training by the priests and older altar servers. He really enjoyed being able to serve at Masses during the week and on Sundays and sometimes at funerals and weddings. It was neat to get out of class and to serve at a weekday funeral. He wasn't stuck in the classroom. How's that coming from a former teacher?

He served until he was a senior in high school. A pastor noticed his zeal for serving and thought that he would make a good priest. The pastor talked about that with him and his family. His parents were okay with it but left it all up to their son. He recalled that his grandparents were really excited about that prospect. The pastor was even willing to pay for his college and seminary tuitions. As it turned out, the young man disappointed his grandparents and the pastor. The reason was that girls were more interesting than the seminary. However, his interest in Holy Mass never wavered. And, as one can surmise, he was eventually led to the Diaconate.

Why Holy Mass?

As he reflected about his time as a young adult, the prayers during Mass, the readings, the Gospel, and the homilies had a profound effect on the way he would think and live. They drew him to the desire to serve, in some way, as an adult, at that altar again. As a result, a priest reached out to him, and, knowing that he was a teacher, asked if he would be interested in becoming a Lector and a Eucharistic Minister. He accepted and went into a brief period of instruction.

As a Lector, he was able to present to the congregation the first and second readings from Holy Scripture, along with sometimes leading the responsorial psalm which falls between the first and second reading, and, when a deacon wasn't present, the intercessory prayers, known more commonly as the prayers of the faithful. For those who may not be familiar with what follows during the Eucharistic Celebration, the first reading is usually from Hebrew Scripture, followed by the psalms, also from Hebrew Scripture, and the second reading is from the New Testament. The Gospel readings are, depending upon the liturgical cycle, from Matthew, Mark, Luke, or John. During the weekday celebrations, the norm is for the first reading to be from the Old Testament and sometimes from the New. This is followed by the responsorial psalm, a Gospel acclamation, and the Gospel. On Special Holy Days, there are two readings, as on Sundays.

As an aside, there are some who think that the Catholic Church is not a Bible-oriented Church. However, if one were to think about the fact that there are three cycles of Scripture readings over a three-year period, one could surmise that if someone were to attend Mass daily, one would have gone through most of the Bible during that time frame.

With that noted, he came to realize that he had listened to Scripture readings for more than 74+ years. For a number of those years, as lector, he had to read them before he presented them to the congregation. Something must have sunk in because that led him to the Diaconate. And, during his five years of preparation for the Diaconate, everyone had to study Holy Scripture along with classes on homiletics.

As a result of reading, meditating, and prayerfully reflecting on the scriptures, he came to realize that what was practiced as a Catholic was always in line with Holy Scripture. This realization led him to believe what some don't want to consider, and that is that Jesus is truly present in the Eucharist. He is present in the Word and the Sacrament and in the people. Many have no problem with His being present in the Word of the Bible, Holy Scripture, and in the people, but some don't think that Jesus is really present in the Host that is consecrated during Holy Mass. They think that it's only a representation or symbol and just part of the remembrance act of the Last

Supper. He respects their thinking. However, the following information is what led him to believe the way he does with respect to that Host truly being the Body, Blood, Soul, and Divinity of Jesus Christ.

After reading, praying about, and meditating on the Gospel of John, chapter 6, especially verses 47-58, the words made sense as to that reality. Then, after reading where many disciples left him because they didn't believe His words, a thought entered as to why Jesus didn't call them back and say to them that He really didn't mean what He said about eating His flesh and drinking His blood, and that it was just symbolic. That really stuck in his mind.

Another thought arose shortly thereafter. If God created the world, the stars, planets, the universe and so many others, why not allow Jesus to be present in the form of bread and wine without people recognizing any change in their substance. It certainly is what the Church calls the Mystery of Faith. The New Testament is full of examples of miracles that Jesus and His disciples performed. Why not this carried out throughout the ages to the present.

As a result of his science background, even after the epiphany about the reality of His presence in the

Eucharist, from time to time he would wonder if his thinking was valid. Therefore, research into Church history followed to see if there were other miracles beyond the Apostolic times that had something to do with the Eucharist. He was not disappointed. There were and are many examples that appear to be truly unexplainable from a scientific point of view. Below, the reader will find a few that really stood out for him.

Miracles of the Eucharist

If the reader were to key in alleged miracles of the Eucharist on the internet, hundreds of examples that occurred over the centuries would be found. One of the most famous happened in Lanciano, Italy, in the eighth century. There are also some that occurred in the 20th and 21st centuries. These happened all over the world, not just in Italy. Some of the strange things that were recorded involved the appearance of blood on Hosts and or in the wine used for Consecration. Others involved the appearance of what looked like various parts of heart tissue and heart muscle.

Some naysayers may point to old science in that 8th-century event, thus criticizing the results. However, modern technology has revealed the truth of what was noted in that century. Science has revealed that in all cases, the blood was human blood, and the heart muscle and tissue was also human. Blood types and DNA testing were also performed, showing the same results from samples all around the world.

For those who may be familiar with the Shroud of Turin, which some believe to be the burial cloth of Jesus, there were matches to samples taken from other alleged miraculous events. One may also find that in certain cases, the scientists who did the testing were not informed of where the samples came from. No prejudice involved.

All these miracles sure seem to lead one to believe that there certainly is a direct relationship to the crucified Jesus. Yet, debunkers use Scripture and their interpretation of it to refute the claims. Some also say that these so-called miracles must be demonic in nature, explaining that such claimants may turn people away from their Catholic belief. However, there appears to be more information that supports belief in the real presence of Jesus in the Eucharist.

A Personal Experience

In his last book, the firefighter/deacon noted a number of alleged Eucharist Miracles that happened at Little Audrey Santo's residence in Worcester, MA. Some information will be revealed here, but details may be found by checking out the Little Audrey Santo Foundation, Inc., website located at https://littleaudreysantofoundation.com/.

The first Host miracle occurred in January of 1992. Others occurred in 1996, 2004, 2010, 2011, 2012, and 2014. The deacon's science background always made him somewhat suspect about how these events could have happened. He had thoughts of the possibility of people placing drops of blood on a paten so that when an unconsecrated Host was placed on top, no one would notice it until it was raised just prior to the Consecration. However, after further investigation and talking with some of the people who were present, he discerned those suspicions were unfounded. Then, on one occasion when he was present as a deacon for presiding priest from Africa, he saw that when the priest raised a host prior to the words of Consecration, drops of blood appeared on the side facing the people. They weren't there until after he raised it up and began the prayers. It sure drew the attention of all who were present. Some naysayers may think that it was an illusion. That would be put down immediately because no one present was an illusionist. Within a few moments of that experience, the host was placed on a separate paten and set on the corporal. A different host was used for the actual Consecration with nothing unusual occurring after that. The blood spotted Host was placed in a tabernacle. Shortly thereafter, that Host began to effuse oil. So, a small bowl was placed there to catch the overflow from the paten.

The 2014 event was entirely different in that a priest who was visiting from Rome and the deacon who experienced it went to look at the previously noted Host. Upon opening the tabernacle, they both noticed that there was an additional Host leaning near the blood spotted Host, and it had oil on it as well as the other one. Both wondered if anyone placed it there to cause yet more excitement. However, it was not likely because the tabernacle was always locked, and only a few people knew where the key was kept. Also, there was no reason to do that because the unexplainable was still going on with oils oozing from pictures and statues within the house, Audrey's room, chapel, and gift shop. There were also changes taking place in a previously blood-soaked Host that was kept in a different tabernacle in the chapel. So, how did that Host get there? Another miracle? Let the reader decide.

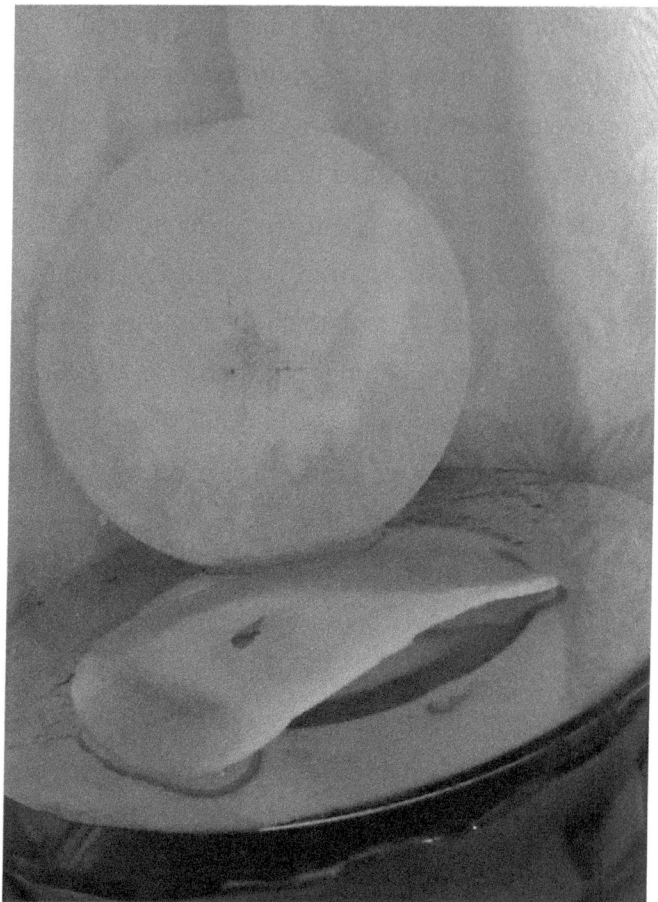

DNA Testing

If the reader was wondering what type of blood appeared on the Host, a reputable company that was used previously to determine if the blood was human or not was called to find out how to go about taking a sample and sending it back to them. The company was BODE Technology. They have done hundreds of thousands of forensic and DNA projects for law enforcement and the FBI.

To make this long story short, the blood samples revealed DNA of Audrey, her mother, Linda, and an unidentifiable female. It was disappointing in a way because most people who were involved with the Foundation were hoping it would be like the findings of the miracles noted earlier in this book. On the plus side, the priest from Rome sent a several page report about the significance of the results. The deacon who witnessed everything interpreted the report in this way: If we are to be part of the Mystical Body of Christ, why not have Audrey's and Linda's blood appear on the Host revealing a connection of love. It sure could be that possibility.

An Overall Positive Effect

Combining all this information about being led to Holy Mass as a youngster, following through with becoming a lector, Eucharistic Minister, and eventually an ordained Deacon, the author of this book came to a conclusion that all that he experienced helped him to be a *better* teacher, firefighter, Fire Chaplain, husband, father, grandfather, son, son in law, brother, brother in law, uncle, and friend to others, and of course, a deacon.

They helped to solidify his thoughts about the importance of Holy Scripture, Holy Mass, and a prayer life that dealt with a personal relationship with Jesus and the effect on him as a person. He would hope that all those with whom he was involved in his life would see him as a person who was loving, caring, nonjudgmental, and willing to help anyone in need. And the experiences also helped him to be able to look for and see Jesus in others. Together, they also kept him from getting a swollen head and, again, helped to realize that he still had faults and failures. He certainly was not perfect. To add a bit of humor to this, he tells people to ask his wife. She would certainly agree that he's not perfect. A good place for a smiley face? 😊

A Prayer Life

In addition to Holy Mass and involvement with Holy Scripture, a prayer life plays an important role in the development of body, mind, and spirit. It has a positive effect in all that we do. Setting time aside for prayer during the day, on a regular basis, can really enhance the well-being of the individual who participates in it. It certainly did for him. However, he didn't realize that until later in life.

As a youngster, his parents taught him how to say the Lord's Prayer, Hail Mary, and Glory Be along with some short prayers involving a Guardian Angel. Also included was praying for mom, dad, his brother, relatives, and others. All prayers were usually practiced before bedtime.

Does the reader remember or has he ever heard of this one? "Angel of God, my guardian dear to whom God's love commits me here, ever this day be at my side, to light and guard, to rule and guide." If not, one may find it and others like it on the internet. The deacon was taught to pray this one every morning. As he got older, he forgot about it because he thought it was just for kids, but over the last ten years

or so, he picked up on it again. His thought was that
it couldn't hurt.

Moving to Something More Involved

There are many people who worry about many things in life, who are anxious, and who are in need of moving through those emotional states to calmness, reduction in stress, and feeling good about themselves. In order to experience that, people resort to Yoga, breathing exercises, use of so-called "worry beads," and the like.

There are those who found such methods to be relaxing and successful. Others have not had the same results and have had to obtain the help of psychologists and/or psychiatrists. Sometimes that last resort is necessary depending upon what the person experienced, how long they were involved with that experienced, and their psychological makeup.

The deacon/fire chaplain lived that trauma for a while after his return from service at the outdoor morgue at Ground Zero in 2001. Praying over dead bodies and body parts played a number on his psyche. Fortunately, his spiritual director, a priest, was also a psychologist. He was able to lead him to peace through a prayer life that included breathing exercises, meditation on Holy Scripture passages during prayer time, attendance at Holy Mass, of course, and the use of the rosary.

The Rosary—A Spiritual Tool

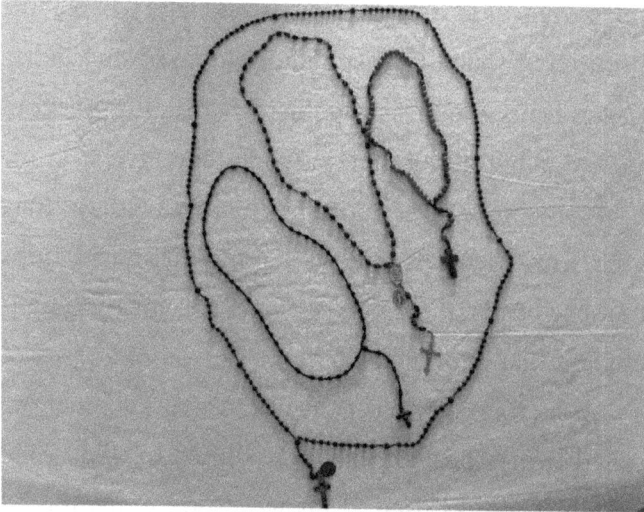

As he was growing up, the deacon occasionally prayed the rosary. However, it was not a daily routine. It was usually prayed in May and October, at least occasionally. In the Catholic Church, May is dedicated to Mary and October to the rosary. Throughout the rest of the year, the deacon prayed the rosary only when he felt an urge to do so. It wasn't until after his Ground Zero experience that he began to pray it on a more regular basis. And, at one point in time, his wife suggested that they pray the rosary together. It is now prayed daily. It helped them in their marital and spiritual lives.

Why would they continue, especially when some groups feel that it is blasphemous to do so since it has pagan roots and is also against what Jesus points out in the Bible about not praying repetitive prayers. Well, anyone can use Scripture to prove truths as they see them. And, yes, there are non-Christian groups that use beads of sorts to pray mantras for their benefit and that of others.

A former teacher acquaintance used what he called "worry beads." They were similar to what some Buddhist monks used. If his words are remembered correctly, he said that by simply fingering them, he could be helped to relax. All that the teacher at the time ever said was, "If it works for you, go for it."

As far as going against what Jesus said in the Gospel of Matthew 67 about not repeating prayers is concerned, the reference there was about people trying to work on the various gods to have them answer the requests as they would want them to. It would be a form of attempted manipulation. The rosary is certainly not that, nor is it to be used in that manner.

First of all, every part of the rosary has its roots in Holy Scripture. Some have a cross on them and others a crucifix. Either one is to remind us of the suffering and death of Jesus and what that means for all of us. The rosary begins with the Apostle's Creed, which is what Christians believe. On the large beads, the prayer would pray Our Lord's prayer, more commonly referred to as the Our Father. On the smaller beads, one prays the Hail Mary. The words are found in the Gospel of Luke. Following the tenth bead, one prays the Glory Be which acknowledges the Triune God, Past, Present, and Future. Some may have also heard people pray the following at the end of each decade. "Oh, my Jesus, forgive us our sins. Save us from the fires of hell. Lead all souls to heaven, especially those most in need of your mercy." It's a beautiful prayer that reminds us of our need for His forgiveness and for us to do our best to stay away from anything that would lead us away from Him. It should also remind us about helping others do likewise. Many have also heard people conclude with a prayer called Hail, Holy, Queen. The deacon especially likes the ending because it asks her to pray for us so that we may become worthy of the promises of

Christ. From time-to-time people ask each other for prayers. Why not ask Jesus's Mother to pray for us to help us to grow closer to God and be worthy of that closeness. Wow.

Catholics refer to a set of mysteries attached to the five sets of ten beads. There are the Glorious mysteries in which the person praying may meditate on the Resurrection, the Ascension, the Decent of the Holy Spirit upon the Apostles, The Assumption of Mary into Heaven, and the Crowning of Mary as Queen of Heaven and Earth. The first three have direct connections to the Bible. The last two are not but are implied in Revelation 12 and other places.

The Joyful Mysteries include the Annunciation, Visitation, The Birth of Jesus, His Presentation in the Temple, and Finding Jesus in the Temple. There is a direct connection to the Gospel of Luke in all five. There's a direct connection to the Gospel of John in the first and to Matthew for the nativity.

The Sorrowful mysteries cover the Agony in the Garden, The Scourging at the Pillar, The Crowning with Thorns, The Carrying of the Cross, and the Crucifixion. There are definite connections here to all four Gospels.

The deacon's favorite to meditate upon are the Luminous Mysteries. The first set of ten involves the Baptism of Jesus, this is followed by the Miracle at the Wedding Feast at Cana, then The Proclamation of the Kingdom. The fourth set is about the Transfiguration. The last set is about the Institution of the Eucharist. These were brought forth by Pope John Paul II in 2002. Anyone who knows even a little about Scripture would acknowledge that these mysteries have a direct connection to the Gospels.

Different Types of Rosaries

There is also a Scriptural Rosary that takes a bit longer to pray. It still covers the basic mysteries as noted previously, but as a person holds each bead, there is a Scriptural passage associated with it. That really helps the individual to reflect upon all that the mystery entails. It also prevents the mind from wandering during the recitation.

Then, there is the rosary prayed through the eyes of Mary. That one can be very moving, especially when done in the presence of a congregation. It's noted here because a female could act as the voice of Mary. The effect is very special and moving upon hearing it. The deacon and his wife did this with a group in attendance. According to those present, her voice made it seem as if Our Blessed Mother was present. They wanted to know when it would be done again. It was prayed again with other women as the voice of Mary. After it was presented, it was deeply appreciated.

Keeping Our Lord's Mother in mind, there is yet another rosary that originated back in the Middle Ages and was rekindled following an apparition in

Kibeho, Africa. It is known as The Seven Sorrows of Mary Rosary. Instead of ten beads in each set, there are only seven. This prayer, "Most Merciful Mother, remind us always of the sorrows of your Son, Jesus" is said at the end of each set.

For those who are familiar with Scripture, it would be easy to recall those times when Mary experienced some scary, anxious, and sad times in her life beginning with the birth of Jesus, events that followed as He was growing up as a child, and, of course, all that lead up to His crucifixion and final burial. For more information, simply check the internet for the Seven Sorrows Rosary. There are several sites that cover the original Middle Ages rosary and about an apparition in Kibeho, Rwanda (a country in Africa) where it was brought to light again.

Continuing with this viewpoint, when a rosary is done in the spirit of meditation and reflection, the recitation of the different mysteries should cause one to focus on the life of Christ, draw one into a closer relationship with Him, and bring about a sense of calmness and peace during the entire prayer and beyond that time frame. Also, from a spiritual standpoint, the experience is very positive because it could also lead to a desire for further exploration of the Bible. And, as noted previously, from a psychological standpoint, when not rushed and when done properly, it is a definite stress reducer. It still reduces stress for the deacon.

The rosary can be prayed anywhere and not just in church, a chapel, or at home. Some would often say the rosary while driving. In a sense, one could look at it as a God-send in that it reduces stress levels, especially when driving in heavy traffic. It beats rising blood pressure and engaging in words and hand gestures that would not be too pleasing to God.

No one in the Catholic Church is forced to pray the rosary. It is always left up to the individual. All the deacon can say is that it works for him as a calming experience, has led him to want to read and reflect on Holy Scripture, and strengthens his desire to deepen his relationship with Our Lord. This, in turn, helped and still helps him to serve others in the state of life that he's involved in.

A Shorter Calming Prayer

With regard to a calming experience and prayer, the deacon's spiritual director introduced him to a simple prayer that has its root in Eastern Orthodoxy. He said that it not only could be used to begin to center himself when there is a desire to meditate, but that it can also be used to diffuse stress in situations involving conversations with people who may be upset with you. The prayer is known as The Jesus Prayer. It goes like this, "Lord Jesus Christ, Son of God, Have Mercy on Me, a Sinner." It can be used as a calming, breathing exercise. On an inhale, one can say, Lord

Jesus Christ. On an exhale one can say, Son of God. On the next inhale one can say, Have Mercy on Me. On the next exhale one can say, a Sinner. Repetition along with breathing aloud or silently can lead to a relaxing event. After reflecting on the words, it is easy to see how it can also be a humbling experience.

After some time using this prayer, the deacon was able to focus better during meditative prayer times. It also came in to play when he was nervous about situations involving doctor visits, dealing with unruly students, when parents were upset with the way he handled grading or behavioral incidents with their sons or daughters, when interacting with fellow firefighters who were upset with him or others in the department, and at times of stressful situations during traumatic experiences, or chaplain-victim encounters as a deacon in his ministry of service to the people, and even during some uptight family situations. The neat thing about it is that no one ever knew what he was doing during the conversations with those involved. Some even asked how he could be so calm during those stressful times. He thanks God for those times. Anger could have taken over, which could have resulted in some serious, negative outcomes for all involved. Knowing this prayer was truly a blessing.

He also adapted that prayer to help him to grow in a closer relationship with God. He would say, "Jesus Christ, Son of God, Help me to Love You More and More." Similar inhaling and exhaling was done with Jesus Christ on the inhale, "Son of God" on the exhale, "Help Me to Love You" on the next inhale, and "More and More" on the exhale. He thinks that it also helped him to focus on being a better Deacon servant. Another thank you goes out for that inspiration.

Ego Building or Not

He once wondered if he was making himself look like a saint so that people would say, "Boy, what a great guy." Or, was he just realizing that all along it wasn't about him, but about God's directing him to people who helped him to become the person that he was at that time. He felt that parents, grandparents, relatives, a loving family, coworkers, clergy, religious, and friends were all gifts from God. All helped to grow, over time, in a positive direction that included Loving God and loving neighbor. It wasn't always a smooth run. It is still a struggle at times to move away from the sins that are not pleasing to God toward a life that is. Without the help of a merciful God, he knew that he couldn't do it. He realized that failure on a regular basis would happen just like anyone else and that he was no better than anyone else. Reminders of not being perfect keep us humble. It was that way throughout his entire life. The following are examples of some humbling experiences.

As a youngster, he thought he was great as a bike rider. He could stand up on the seat and ride several feet with hands outstretched. Then one day while showing off, he lost balance, fell, and had injuries that took a great deal of time to heal. The dumb show off got his due.

As an eighth grader, he was elected to be a patrol boy and would help kids cross the street at an intersection that he was assigned to. He wasn't supposed to stop cars like a police officer would, but from time to time he would. One time, he noticed that his older cousin was driving by. He not only stopped her car but also jumped to sit on the hood as the youngsters crossed the street. When he slid off, he ripped his pants on the hood ornament, and everyone laughed because they could see his underwear. That spread throughout the school. Can you imagine what hearing the following did for his psyche: "Hey, it's the great patrol boy. Have you sat on any car hoods lately?"

He also thought that he was a pretty good football player even though he didn't play for a team. However, he quickly found out the opposite when a high school player joined up on a private field and did a simple down field block. It took that great player, the future deacon, a while to get up. He then knew that he was not as good as once thought and that there was more for him to learn. Ouch.

At an early age, he learned how to water ski. He felt pretty good being able to slalom. He could go side to side and jump the wakes pretty well. On one occasion, the showoff leaned out too far and too close to the water. That resulted in at least a twenty-five-foot log roll. There were a lot of cheers heard along the shoreline. That feat was never tried again.

And, how about a captain of a Ladder Company who forgot to follow his own instructions to constantly check on the equipment. Once, while on the Aerial Ladder truck's 75-foot extension, the ladder wasn't locked properly, and he got his foot caught between the rungs. He had to pull his foot out of his boot and move down with only one on. The great captain got a bit of heckling for a long time after that.

Sometimes from the mouths of children come some heart-wrenching words. Once, after reading Scripture during Mass, the lector went out to the car where his family was waiting. After he got in the car, he noticed that the car was boxed in and couldn't move. The nice lector had a few choice words to say about those people whom he judged to be very inconsiderate. His children said that he should practice what he just read in Church and be kind, not angry. That sunk in. It never happened again. Every time anything similar happened, he remembered the wise words of his kids.

It didn't end there. As a deacon, he once proclaimed the wrong Gospel during a Confirmation service in the presence of a new Bishop. He dropped Hosts. He spilled sacramental wine. He knocked over altar candles. He forgot to light incense for a special service. He read the wrong name for people during the intercessory prayers. And, from time to time, he would trip over his alb and even ripped a stole. And every so often he would hear a parishioner say, just before Mass, "Hey Deacon, you forgot to light the candles." He thanked God for those humbling experiences. Remembering them keeps him real and less judgmental about others.

No One is Perfect

No one is perfect. Even the best of them. After reading several stories about different saints, the deacon realized that they too were not perfect. They even considered themselves to be sinners. They prayed daily that they wouldn't fall into sin. Their faith was strong as well as their trust in God. Many even gave up their lives rather than give up their Christian beliefs and are known as martyrs.

There was one saint who really impressed him regarding his worrying about falling away from his belief in Jesus and the Real Presence in the Eucharist. His name is Padre Pio, now recognized as Saint Padre Pio. He was known for his gift of being able to be in two places at once, which is called bilocation. He also had what is called the Stigmata. He had holes in his hands, feet, and side. The most prominent were in his hands. He had them wrapped while he was presiding at Holy Mass. St. Pio was also known for his special insight into the thoughts of people who came to confess their sins. Many healings were attributed to him while he was alive and after his death.

Even with all that Padre Pio was involved with, he was concerned about the possibility of moving away from the truth of the Gospels. Because of that, he came up with a prayer pleading with Jesus never to leave him. It is called the "Stay With Me Prayer." He wanted Jesus to always remain with him because he felt that it was so easy for him to let Jesus go due to his own personal, frail humanity. St. Pio felt that it was difficult for him to stay focused on Jesus like he wanted to. Therefore, he developed this prayer so that he could say it after receiving Holy Communion. He didn't trust himself, therefore he asked Jesus, as noted previously, to always remain with him. The prayer may be found on a website devoted to his life and work:

https://www.padrepiodapietrelcina.com/en/
stay-with-me-lord-padre-pio-prayer/

Prayers, Books, and Booklets

There are many different prayers, books, and booklets that can help us to become better in whatever state of life we find ourselves. Instructions and training on the secular aspects of our lives are a must. Continuous on-the-job training is also important. And there are also courses and information available to assist us with the psychological aspects of our lives. Some people even exercise daily, either at a gym or at home to promote good body health. And there are plenty of books, CDS, DVDS, television, and online information to assist us in that regard.

The good thing is that there are also just as many opportunities to build up our spiritual lives. Many don't seem to realize that when our spiritual life is in good order it has a positive effect on everything else. When there is a good balance within body, mind, and spirit, we seem to do better when dealing with loved ones in our families, with coworkers, friends, and people in general no matter where we are. The deacon realized that as he grew older that this has helped all the way around and especially in his teaching career, as a Captain of a Ladder Company, and as a Deacon.

He always thanked God for helping him to grow in that regard.

One of the booklets that has helped a great deal is entitled, "My Saint Pio Prayer Booklet" from the Padre Pio Foundation of America. The shrine is located in Cromwell, Connecticut. The booklet contains 24 pages of the basic prayers, noted previously, along with many others that focus on Our Lord and are very uplifting. It is here that the deacon found the prayer, "Stay with Me, Lord."

Another booklet was given to him by Linda Santo, the mother of Audrey Santo. Linda is a Roman Catholic and also a member of the Maronite Church. The booklet is a Novena to Saint Charbel Makhlouf. Saint Charbel was born in Lebanon and was a priest and member of the Lebanese Maronite Order. Many miracles are attributed to his intercession. The booklet is only fifteen pages, including the basic prayers and the Ten Commandments. It has helped the deacon focus on his own needs and those of others, which has offered the opportunity to pray for those needs. Information about this saint may be found online. His story is really interesting.

Another booklet used daily is published by the Divine Mercy Department, Marian Helpers Center, Congregation of Marians, Stockbridge, MA. It is only 80 pages in length. It is entitled *Devotion to The Divine Mercy*. The deacon found it to be particularly interesting because the authors point out that the information within it is for private recitation and that the purpose of the devotion to The Divine Mercy is to prepare the world for the Lord's return. Another reason that it piqued his interest is that some of the information comes from the diary revelations of a Polish nun, Sister Faustina Kowalska. The deacon's Polish family members were excited when they heard about all that Sister Faustina presented in her diary.

When he returned to Webster for various occasions to serve at St. Joseph's Basilica, the deacon always enjoyed looking at the huge painting of Jesus, the Divine Mercy. He is in the usual garment with red and white rays coming from His heart. The words "Jesus, I trust in You" are visible in Polish, "Jezu Ufam Tobie."

The deacon will never forget those words because a deacon friend gave him a stone cutting with them engraved in it. It is strategically placed in front of a

Marian shrine area in their yard. It made sense to place it there because Mary always points to her son, Jesus, wants us always to turn to Him, and remind us always of His Divine Mercy. It makes sense because if we do trust in Him and follow through with what He has taught us, in whatever state of life we find ourselves, we won't have to worry about any "End Times," whether they be personal or for everyone, whenever that may occur in the future.

The End or New Beginnings?

As the deacon/chaplain looks at where he is now and what he has been able to do in the past, he comes to the conclusion that he has been guided along the way through all his various states of life. He truly believes that it was only by the grace of God that he was able to do what he did in all his stages of his life. He is also thankful that many of his past thoughts, words, and actions didn't get him into serious trouble.

This would also be a good time to note that one of the greatest gifts in his life that God gave him was his wife, Alice. He considers her to be a very holy, loving, caring person. Her interest in Holy Mass, personal prayer, the saints, and the rosary has kept her going through many difficult times in her life, especially when it involved the loss of one son at birth, and their oldest when he was fifty years old, and also regarding the pain involved with over thirty-three operations on various parts of her body. She would always remind her husband to be sure to have her rosary in the hospital room after surgery and that the staff would be notified that she was Catholic and would like to receive Holy Communion when possible. She was and still is a definite inspiration. Without her as a special gift, the deacon doesn't think he would have been able to have grown into the person that he is today. He thanks God daily for His beautiful gift.

We could end this short work here, but someone reminded the author of this book that people would probably like to know how the deacon got to this point in time and whether or not things were pretty normal as he grew up. Therefore, the following paragraphs will go back in time for a while to hopefully help the reader see how this all grew together from early childhood to adulthood.

Some Early Childhood Events

The deacon remembers a time in his early child-hood when his parents would reprimand him for doing things that were not that good. On one occasion, his mother got angry with him because he crawled under the ironing board while she was ironing some clothes. That wasn't all of it. He thought it would be funny if he pulled the plug that was attached to the iron to see the expression on his mother's face. The result was not what he expected and not pleasing to him at all. Why? Because as he grabbed the plug that was attached to the socket and pulled hard on it, he touched the metal parts and got the shock of his life. As a result of that, he went flying backwards from beneath the ironing board, knocking it over along with the iron that was on top. The iron fell on the floor and burned a part of the rug near where it was standing. A lesson was surely learned, but it didn't end there. His mother pulled him aside, raised her voice, and set him in the corner of the room. He, in his non-saintly manner, slapped her legs. The age-old saying of "Wait till your father gets home," rang over and over in his mind. Fear set in because he knew that his dad would follow through with something painful. Well, after his father arrived and the story was told, there was a spanking involved along with his not being able to watch television for quite some time. Would Howdy Doody miss this child? Most would agree that the puppet certainly would not miss him.

In this day and age, in many circles, spankings would certainly be frowned upon. Reality proves it with some parents being brought up on abuse charges and children being removed from those homes. However, back then spanking was normal discipline. That's what people were accustomed to. One must also realize that there certainly can be a difference between spanking and beating although in some cases it would be a close call. Usually, spanking did not result in bruised or swollen body parts and visual black and blue marks. An occasional slight slap on the hand or a few taps on the bottom end may have been painful, but not critical. And, as a result, lessons were often learned, and the behavior that supposedly warranted them would hopefully never be repeated. In this instance of the iron, it never again happened.

One may wonder if spanking affected him over time in how he would discipline his own children. To

settle any curiosity, he did spank his children on occasion, but fortunately those times were few and far
between. Since those times, he regrets that they even
were considered. He thanks God that as he matured,
his behavior changed for the better. Spanking was replaced with common sense, firm conversations that
hopefully gave his children important facts to keep in
mind and that would help them to become better human beings.

On a lighter side, the now deacon said that he is
glad that as a youngster he didn't know too much
about Scripture. If he had, there would have been no
way for him to follow the verse about turning the
other cheek. He would have asked himself if our Lord
was referring to the cheeks on one's face or those that
made up the buttocks. Either way, it would have hurt,
and he knew that pain was not a welcome neighbor.
He now realizes that it wouldn't have made much difference to God because God knows the limitations of
children and adults. He also thanks God for realizing
that God's love and mercy knows no bounds.

More Lessons Learned The Hard Way

Fortunately for the young child who learned not to play with an electrical outlet, other interesting events got him to think about how he was saved from serious injuries. Could a Guardian Angel have been involved? Maybe so.

As he grew older into a pre-pubescent followed by years of puberty, his interest led him into the areas of science and technology. It was somewhere around the time when he was in the eighth and ninth grades that he thought chemistry would be the way to go. Following a great deal of talk about how many of his friends had chemistry sets, his parents got him one as part of his Christmas presents. Mom and dad gave him specific instructions as to when and where he could use it.

The young chemistry student had to read all the instructions carefully, report to mom and dad that he knew what he was doing, and only then was he able to work on a particular experiment. During that time, the young chemist was allowed to perform the experiments in the basement of their home. That lasted until a foul, sulfury odor waffled its way up into the dining room, living room, and den on the first floor above the basement. A rotten egg smell just didn't cut it in a home that always smelled clean or held the wonderful aroma that came from good old-fashioned home cooking. As a result, the young chemist and his chemistry set were moved to an outdoor shed.

Even though he had to move, he was excited because he had more room to work. There was a work bench that was approximately eight feet long with shelving behind it and beneath it where he could keep his chemicals and other materials.

The original instructions by mom and dad still had to be adhered to. The instructions were followed until the young chemist thought that he was now old enough and mature enough to experiment on his own. He thought, "My goodness, me, I'm a high school freshman and taking science classes, so I should be able to do what I want, when I want."

A new lesson was to be learned after he began to experiment with chemicals that were not in his chemistry set. These chemicals could produce smoke. The chemicals were similar to those that would go into making gun powder. Tiny smoke bombs were one thing. However, he found out that making small firecrackers was an advanced skill that he thought would become fun for himself and his friends.

At one point, one of his uncles found out about his interest in chemistry and gave him some metallic ribbon that would burn with a bright white light. His uncle worked in a place where that ribbon was used for a particular purpose. The ribbon was magnesium. His uncle often used it to demonstrate how light energy can be produced and how one must be careful during the demonstration.

The nephew was deeply appreciative of that small gift. Once again, his dad told him to be extremely careful when it was used and that it could only be used out of doors and nowhere near any buildings. Well, as one may surmise, that advice lasted only for a short time. Now, the Master Chemist, or so he thought of himself, was going to use pieces of the ribbon as wicks for his miniature fireworks.

That was short-lived when he tried to make a much larger firecracker. The wick burned faster than he anticipated. It burned so hot and fast that the firecracker blew up prematurely. The Master Chemist ended up with a blackened face, singed eyebrows, and a funny looking hair line. That experience ended his experimentation with smoke bombs and fire cracker-related materials. Looking back again on his life, he wondered if Guardian Angels were involved.

Goodbye Chemistry, Hello...?

So, what do you think replaced his interest in chemistry? Believe it or not, he began to lean towards the field of electronics. Maybe the early childhood shock had a long term effect. However, reality dictated his thinking, and his interest was more likely because his father was adept at repairing lamps and other household items like toasters, small heaters, radios, and even television sets. His dad also was able to rewire parts of their home and wire the garage and work area in the shed. The interest most likely rubbed off on him because he began thinking that he just might be able to follow in his father's footsteps.

His dad was pleased with his son's interest and not only gave him some books to read, but also gave him some personal, hands-on instruction. As a result, when it came time to present a project for one of his science classes, he designed some models showing the difference between Alternating and Direct Current circuits. He and a friend put the models together. The models involved some wiring, switches, light bulbs, batteries, and the like.

His high school science teacher was impressed and complimented him and his friend for an assignment well done. The humorous side of this wanna be electrician ended the demonstration by saying to his teacher, "Seeing that you really enjoyed our demonstration, how about no homework for the class this weekend." The class burst into laughter and applause. After composing himself, the teacher smiled and agreed to a limited amount of homework. Smiley face anyone? Maybe a groan?

By the way, that science teacher was influential in piquing that student's interest in science to the point of his desiring to become a science teacher himself. As a result, he eventually applied to a teacher's college and was admitted, graduating from Worcester State College in 1966.

Even though he became a science teacher and not an electrician, he was able, with the help of his cousin, who had a background in electronics, to wire the house that he, his wife, and his family would live in for many years. The building and wiring inspectors passed the work with flying colors. The teacher/ firefighter thanked his dad for all that he taught him. He also thanks Jesus for the guidance and intelligence to get to that point in time successfully.

Back to High School for a Moment

Even though his interest in science and electricity were a part of his life, they were to some degree put on the back burner as well. That most likely was the result of what some may consider a normal maturing process that happens around the age of puberty.

Different sparks began to fly, which were due to his interest in girls. Prior to that time during elementary and junior high school, girls were a no, no. In his mind they were silly, weak, and to be kept at a distance. He frowned upon going to any parties where girls were present because all they seemed to want to do was to play silly games and talk about movies and movie stars. However, by tenth grade he noticed that a number of guys that he hung around with had girl friends, and they appeared to be happy hanging around them. His eyes were opened, and he eventually got up enough courage to ask girls out on dates. Often, movies were involved. How about that?

He was not always successful, but he did notice that some of the girls smiled back and were okay with his approach. A few dances, beach parties at the local lake and ponds were fun. During the latter part of his senior year, someone told him that there was a neat-looking girl who kept eyeing him from time to time. One thing led to another. They began to date, fell in love, and wanted to continue with a lasting relationship. A problem would occur when both went to different colleges. Time spent apart began to work on their relationship and after a year or so the girl found someone else more attractive and interesting. His heart was broken, but life moved on. An interesting event followed in that his old girl friend's family embraced him and invited him to hang around with them. To some degree, it helped to ease the heartache, and over time healing took place.

That family even accepted his new girlfriend with open arms, and many good times followed. The reader may wonder where this is all going. One may begin to realize that all this was part of God's plan for this girl and the future firefighter/deacon. Guess where they met, it was during their Junior year at Worcester State College. Did God, math, and science come together in this relationship? Looking back at that time in his life, it sure looked that way.

This girl had a very strong religious background and seemed to also be gifted in the sense that she had a real relationship with Jesus and the Blessed Mother.

She would go to Holy Mass on a regular basis. No one had to tell her or force her to go even at an early age. During the Lenten Season, she would often stop into a church after school to pray for herself, her family, and her friends. During her college years, she would do the same. At one time during her college years, because there were no dorms at that time, she stayed with a family and was involved with taking care of their four children. On occasion she would tutor them when they asked for help. Walking two miles to church and two miles back was somewhat tiring. She felt that all that walking had a good side because it helped her to remain a slim young lady.

The family that she lived with would also take ski vacations in Vermont. During bad weather, they would drive her to Holy Mass. That family was not Catholic, but they appreciated who she was, the work she did for the family, and her devout Catholicism.

The reader should certainly be able to see how God, most likely, had been involved with this match. The result led to their marriage after college graduation in 1966. Their oldest child came into the world over a year later. He was followed by their second son a little over a year after that. Those were two blessed moments in their lives that brought them much joy.

Now it would be their turn to teach their children how to bless themselves and say their prayers, and to tell them why Holy Mass was important.

A few years later, their third child was lost because of complications just before his expected birth date. How fortunate he was that the Catholic doctor who was to bring him into the world baptized him immediately. Sadness surely followed. It was tough for this future deacon to leave his wife to recover in the hospital and bury his baby boy with only a friend and priest present. He and his wife thanked God for friends who understood their situation and were there to support them with their presence and prayers.

After a while and following much prayer, his wife felt in her heart that she would like to have another child. As a result, a beautiful daughter was brought into the world. Her two older brothers were thrilled when she was born, and they always took good care of her. It was always a great Sunday when the entire family made it to church and were all seated in the same pew.

Life continued with the usual years that involved good and not so good days. Sicknesses and stressful situations that most teenagers face came about. Both parents made it through those times and know in their hearts and minds that it was everyone's relationship with our Lord that got them through in a positive manner. They are proud of their children who now have children of their own. Great grandchildren are now part of their family life. Prayers continue on a daily basis for all to get to know Jesus and to follow his ways and to grow in a closer relationship with Him. Time will tell. The prayers never stop.

With all that noted previously, he sincerely hopes that he did his best to do what is considered right living. He hopes that if he did offend people that they forgave him for his transgressions. He also hopes that, as a result of his words and actions, he didn't turn people off from growing closer to God. For him, that would be really bad. Fortunately, however, he does trust in Jesus and His forgiveness. That trust helps the author to continue his life in a positive manner. He is confident that guided opportunities will arise to do good. New beginnings are always appreciated. He hopes that he will always remember and act upon what we often hear at the end of the celebration of The Holy Eucharist, "Go in peace, glorifying the Lord, by your life."

May whoever reads this book be granted the graces to always do good, avoid evil in any form, to grow closer to Our Lord, and to lead a peaceful life that will do exactly what the title asks us all to do.